THE CHANGING FACE OF
CZECH
REPUBLIC

Text by JACOB ŘIHOŠEK
Photographs by JENNY MATTHEWS

WAYLAND

© 2004 White-Thomson Publishing Ltd

Produced for Hodder Wayland by
White-Thomson Publishing Ltd
2/3 St Andrew's Place
Lewes BN7 1UP

Editor: Elaine Fuoco-Lang
Designer: Clare Nicholas
Concept Design: Chris Halls, Mind's Eye Design
Consultant: Christopher Sadil
Proofreader: Philippa Smith

First published in Great Britain in 2004 by Hodder Wayland, an imprint of
Hodder Children's Books.

This paperback edition published in 2007 by Wayland
an imprint of Hachette Children's Books.

British Library Cataloguing in Publication Data
Řihošek, Jacob
    The Changing Face of the Czech Republic
    1. Human geography – Czech Republic – Juvenile literature
    2. Czech Republic – History – Juvenile literature 3. Czech
    Republic – Social life and customs – Juvenile literature
    I. Title II. Czech Republic
    943.7'105

ISBN-13: 978 0 7502 5109 9

Printed in China

Wayland,
an imprint of Hachette Children's Books
338 Euston Road, London NW1 3BH

Acknowledgements
The publishers would like to thank
the following for their contributions
to this book: Rob Bowden – statistics
research; Peter Bull – map
illustration; Nick Hawken – statistics
panel illustrations. Thanks also to
Tomas Řihošek for translations and
Jenny Matthews for the interviews.
All photographs are by Jenny
Matthews except: Corbis/Jonathan
Blair 10 (top), Corbis/Liba Taylor
23 (top); Joe Klamar/Reuters/
Popperfoto.com 9 (top),
Sue Ogrocki/Reuters/Popperfoto.com
33 (top).

Contents

1 The Capital

For more than a thousand years, Prague has been the biggest city and the centre of government of the country now known as the Czech Republic. In ancient times, Prague was home to the Czech kings. Today the president lives in Hradcany Castle overlooking the Vltava, the city's main river. The city's location, in the centre of the country, has played an important role in its trade. Prague's markets were renowned as the biggest and the richest in the country. Wenceslas Square, named after the first Christian ruler of the Czechs, was once home to a horse fair; today it is one of the city's biggest tourist attractions.

For much of the twentieth century, the ruling Communist Party made access to Prague difficult for some foreign visitors. However, since major political changes occurred after the fall of the Communist government in 1989 (see page 6) tourism has become one of the Czech Republic's main industries. Visitors from all over the world come to see Prague's stunning architecture and view the superb collection of art in its many galleries.

Most of the changes seen in Prague since 1989 have begun to spread to the rest of the country; foreign businesses are investing in the Czech Republic and the country is undergoing great modernisation and change.

▲ *The Hradcany Castle in Prague now serves as a Presidential Palace. A special flag is raised when the president is present.*

◀ *A supermarket building in central Prague. After 1989 many of the capital's streets were modernized.*

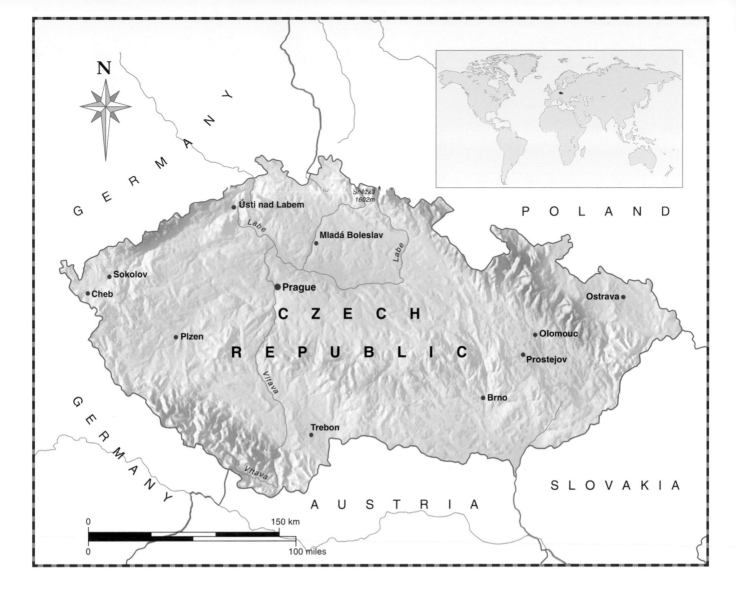

▲ This map shows the main geographical features of the Czech Republic as well as most of the places mentioned in this book.

THE CZECH REPUBLIC: KEY FACTS

Area: 78,866 sq km

Population: 10.3 million

Population density: 130 people per sq km

Capital city: Prague

Other main cities: Brno (0.38 million), Plzen (0.16 million), Ostrava (0.33 million)

Highest mountain: Snezka (1,602 m)

Longest river: Vltava (430 km)

Main language: Czech

Major religions: Atheist 39.8 per cent, Roman Catholic 39.2 per cent, Protestant 4.6 per cent, Orthodox 3 per cent, other 13.4 per cent

Currency: 1 Czech Crown = 100 halers

Past Times

The Czech Republic was once part of Czechoslovakia, a federation (combination) of the Czechs and the Slovaks. The two countries joined in 1918. In 1948, Czechoslovakia became part of the Eastern Bloc, a group of countries dominated by the Soviet Union. There was little contact allowed with Western Europe and all companies were controlled by the Communist government, which remained in power from 1948 until 1989.

▲ *Statues of workers from the post-war era can be seen in the Museum of Communism in Prague.*

During this period most Czechs and Slovaks felt restricted by the government in many areas of their lives. For example, it wasn't easy to get a good job without being a member of the Communist Party. People couldn't freely express different political views without the danger of being prosecuted by the Communist regime. The year 1968 was the most difficult period of the post-war history of the Czech Republic. A strong movement by the people, against the authority of Moscow, was repressed by the invading Soviet armies. Although there wasn't an armed conflict many activists of the movement were imprisoned. After this people became afraid to raise their voices again. In the late 1980s the power of the Soviet Union was beginning to fall and many people decided that it was time for a change. And so in 1989, after a peaceful street protest in Prague, the Communist Party gave way to a more democratic system. This marked an important change in Czechoslovakian politics and economy.

▼ *The famous astronomical clock of Prague. This major tourist attraction was built in AD 1410 and is still functioning today.*

New opportunities opened up for trading with countries in the West. The effects on Czech society were far reaching. The differences between social classes became more apparent and have continued to increase. The latest major change in Czech history took place in 1992 when, after a mutual agreement, the federation of Czechoslovakia was split into the Czech Republic and the Slovak Republic, as they are today.

▶ *The Marks & Spencer supermarket branch in central Prague is an example of how foreign businesses expanded in the Czech Republic after 1989.*

IN THEIR OWN WORDS

'My name is Jan Řihošek. I am optimistic for our children. They will be a happier generation without the experience of 1948 when the Communist government took over, or 1968 when the Russians occupied us. I was so surprised when the Revolution happened in 1989 – I never thought it would be possible to change the socialist regime.

Now there are great changes happening in our country. One positive change is that children now have good environmental education. I run a sports shop selling skateboards, snowboards, windsurfing boards and sailing equipment. Western sports have become very popular with the younger generation. However, even in these changing times it is hard to survive economically as I have to compete with other shops and rely on young people having enough money to spend.'

3 Landscape and Climate

The Czech Republic is a small, landlocked country in the heart of the European continent. It is located on some of the oldest and most significant land routes in Europe. The country doesn't have any coastline but shares its borders with four other countries; Poland in the north, Slovakia in the east, Austria in the south and Germany in the west.

◄ The lack of coastline means that all the areas of water in the Czech Republic are fresh water. Most of the slow-moving sections of the rivers freeze over when temperatures drop in winter.

▼ The spring in the Czech Republic brings a dramatic change to the landscape. The bare trees and yellow grass are replaced by greenery.

The seasons

From the north of the Czech Republic to the south is only a few hundred kilometres so the weather conditions and temperatures are very similar all over the country. The weather in the Czech Republic is affected by two very different climates. The oceanic weather systems coming from the west bring humid weather from the Atlantic, whereas the easterly winds off the Asian continent are drier, and very cold in winter. There are four clearly defined seasons. The normal summer temperature is around 26 °C. In winter it varies between −11 °C and 0 °C, although the temperatures are even lower in the mountains.

Flooding

In recent years there has been more rain in the summer months than ever before. Scientists believe that this is happening because the world climate is becoming warmer. As a result the Czech Republic has recently seen the most destructive floods in recorded history. Floods that have happened in the past few years have caused billions of pounds worth of damage. During the floods in 2002, which also affected Germany and Austria, the water level rose so high in Prague that it flooded the underground system. Many people were also left homeless after their houses collapsed.

▶ *The floods in Prague in 2002 caused the river Vltava to rise dramatically, which badly damaged the city.*

IN THEIR OWN WORDS

'I'm Tomas Řihošek, I was born in Olomouc but I have been living in Prague for the last two years. The climate in the Czech Republic is pretty balanced with warm summers and cold snowy winters. People say it is getting warmer but it is hard to tell. I have seen two floods, in 1997 and in 2002. In Olomouc in 1997, it rained for three months and flooded my dad's shop and nearly ruined his business. In 2002 people took more notice because it affected Prague and transport was badly disrupted – the Metro closed down for six months. Around the river Vltava in Prague, drainage tunnels are being built. Some of the flooding has occurred because forests have been cut down. The soil has eroded away and rivers have been diverted from their natural courses. This is so that farmers have dry fields all year round and housing can be built on the flood plain.'

Forests

Forests and woodland cover 34 per cent of the Czech Republic. There are areas, especially in the north, where trees and soil have suffered damage due to acid rain. The government has taken big steps to try to improve the quality of air, including introducing stricter laws to reduce emissions. The levels of sulphur dioxide, the main chemical responsible for acid rain, are now ten times less than in 1987.

Rivers and lakes

The Czech Republic has many lakes and rivers. Only a few lakes are natural and these are of glacial origin and can be found in the mountains. Glacial lakes were created during the last Ice Age when massive glaciers pushed through the valleys and melted into lakes. Most lakes are dams. The dams are used as drinking water reservoirs and to generate hydro-electricity. The biggest dam, called Lipno, is on the Vltava river in the south of the country.

▲ *Decades of acid rain have destroyed these Norway Spruce trees. It could take more than 200 years for the soil to recover.*

The Labe river is not as long as the Vltava but it is wider and deeper. It provides a shipping connection between the port of Usti nad Labem in the north and the North Sea.

▶ *Summertime is a welcome opportunity for Prague's visitors to explore the Vltava river on hired watercraft.*

Mountains

There are many different mountain ranges, mostly along the border regions. The highest mountain is Snezka at 1,602 m. It is one of the Krkonose Mountains in the north. In the south-west, the Sumava range is where the river Vltava has its source. There are many national reserves in the mountains with scenic landscapes, castle ruins and a lot of beautiful woodland and protected wildlife species. Most of the forests can be found in the mountains, where they consist mainly of coniferous trees.

► *Most of the forested areas are found in the mountain regions of Olomouc.*

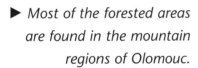

IN THEIR OWN WORDS

'I'm Eva Martinková and I belong to the Czech Union of Environmentalists, which is a non-governmental organization that arranges activities like cleaning up rivers and planting new forests. Groups like ours are allowed to intervene if a law is broken and demand that it is put right. For example, yesterday I came across a man who had ploughed a field where there is a protected iris. I told him he had to return the meadow to its original state or he'll be taken to court.

The main change to the environment is that controls on air pollution caused by the coal power plants have been introduced. Although there are more cars causing pollution, they are mainly in the cities and on the motorways, whereas the coal plants were sited across the whole country.'

4

Natural Resources

Energy sources

In the Czech Republic most energy is currently produced from coal. The coal is burnt in huge quantities to provide the country with more than 70 per cent of its electricity. Nuclear power production is not so developed and provides only 20 per cent of energy. The Czech Republic produces only small quantities of oil and mainly relies on importing oil from Russia. The Czech Republic has built a pipeline (the Ingolstadt-Kralupy pipeline) to carry oil from the Adriatic Sea to the Czech Republic. Other energy sources include hydro-electric power, wind and solar power. These alternative energy sources are the most ecological but currently produce only a fraction of the energy needed. This is because they only began to be used after the fall of the Communist government and they are still in development.

▲ *Most of the electricity in the Czech Republic is produced by coal-powered plants.*

IN THEIR OWN WORDS

'My name is Sylva Joukalová and I'm studying to be a biology teacher in Olomouc. The landscape of the Czech Republic has changed a lot since 1989, with many more houses and roads being built. Olomouc itself is growing and areas that were fields are now covered by supermarkets. But places where there used to be rubbish have been cleaned up and made into play areas for children. Now there are parks for children and special bins for people to clean up after their dogs. In the 1970s and 1980s the Krusne Hory Forest was almost destroyed because of acid rain, due to the prevailing winds blowing from the factories. After 1989 some of the factories were closed down and filters were put on chimneys of those left open, and now the forests are flourishing again.'

Mining

Although reserves are limited, black and brown coal is still produced in large quantities. The largest coalfields are found in the north-east near Ostrava and in the extreme west near Sokolov. Open-pit mining methods are used to extract the brown coal, and this has a devastating effect on the landscape. Land which has been mined using the open-pit method is called 'moonscape' because the land is bare like the surface of the moon.

The Czech Republic has limited sources of metallic ores, namely iron, lead and zinc. There is a source of gold just south of Prague but mining there is banned because it would cause too much damage to the environment.

▲ *Open-pit mining methods have scarred the landscape around Sokolov in the west of the country.*

◄ *The western region of the Czech Republic provides this special type of clay, called kaolin. It is being taken to a factory to be used to make porcelain and ceramics.*

Fish production

Although the Czech Republic is landlocked, it produces significant amounts of freshwater fish. More than 23,000 lakes and ponds have been built for industrial fishing. The most important fish farming area is the Trebon district in the south of the country where more than 70 per cent of the ponds are located. The fish farmers use natural foods, rather than artificial feeding, to achieve better results in fish breeding. The common carp accounts for more than 85 per cent of fish production. In Czech cuisine, battered carp served with potato salad is an important part of the traditional Christmas meal.

▲ Fillets of carp on display in a fishmonger's shop. Most of the carp breeding ponds are in the Trebon district in the south of the country.

◀ Sport fishing is allowed in most areas provided it's done at the right time of the year, and all fishermen must have a valid fishing licence.

Timber resources

The Czech forests and woodland cover one-third of the country. The number of trees planted is greater than the number that are cut down, to make sure that the forests are maintained. Large areas of forest can be damaged in winter storms, when the wind is so strong that it breaks even bigger trees.

Most of the timber is softwood from trees like pine or fir. Wood is an important material for building, furniture and paper production. Experiments are being carried out using hemp fibre for paper production instead of wood, because hemp produces more paper than trees grown on the same area of land and it also takes less time to grow.

▼ *Trees that have been cut down are taken to the nearest railway station before being loaded onto a train for further distribution.*

IN THEIR OWN WORDS

'My name is Jiří Petrášek. At the moment I'm unemployed, but I used to be in charge of production in a timber yard that made doors and windows. Before the Revolution the woods were owned by the state. Then, after 1989, they went back to private ownership, to people who didn't have any experience of managing forests. Some of them just wanted to make money and so they chopped all of the trees down and sold them, particularly for export. There was no control. Our company needed very big trees to work with, but now timber in the Czech Republic is too expensive even for the foreign market – they buy it from Latvia and Lithuania. Now I'm hoping to get another job in a different timber yard, but it's hard for people in their fifties to find work.'

Agriculture

Only 11 per cent of Czechs are employed in agriculture. However, 40 per cent of the land in the Czech Republic is used as arable land. The main plant products are grains (for making bread), potatoes, sugar beet, hops and fruit. Bread and potatoes are an important part of the traditional Czech diet.

◄ *Almost half of the country is used as arable land. This is possible because the flat landscape is ideal for growing crops.*

▼ *The number of people who work in the agriculture industry has declined greatly since the 1960s.*

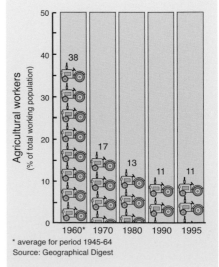

Agricultural workers
(% of total working population)

50
40
30
20
10
0

38
17
13
11
11

1960* 1970 1980 1990 1995
* average for period 1945-64
Source: Geographical Digest

Hops are important for the brewing industry. The brewing industry has seen big drops in the number of breweries. At the beginning of the twentieth century there were more than 600 breweries in the Czech Republic. However, many of the smaller companies have been taken over by competitors and there are now only about 80 breweries in the country.

South Moravia, in the south-east of the Czech Republic, is the warmest part of the country where some wine grapes are grown that produce a good quality white wine.

In Communist times, the Czech agricultural system used to run on the basis of 'collective agricultural teams'. Each one of these teams was a self-sufficient farm. Every five and ten years the government set production targets that determined how many crops were to be produced in a set period of time. The Communist system was not very focused on protecting the environment and as a result a lot of artificial fertilizers were used on the soil. Today, farming has changed from being government-run to privately-run with more focus on protecting the environment. The food grown on the environmentally-friendly farms of today is now becoming popular. People appreciate the difference in its taste and nutritional value, as well as the effect on the environment, compared to food grown on a large scale using artificial fertilizers.

▲ *Many modern organic farms now keep fewer animals and focus more on their well-being.*

IN THEIR OWN WORDS

'I'm Michal Polák. At the present I'm doing my military service, but as soon as I've finished I want to work on an organic farm. At the moment Europe is over-producing food, which needs to be managed better. Some people aren't interested in organic food as they prefer to pay for cheaper non-organic products, so it's hard for our organic farmers to compete. There are two types of farms here – small-scale ones whose owners want to get the best from their land and sell in the local markets, and the enormous intensive farms, the remnants of the Communist regime, which damage the environment but which supply the supermarkets with cheap, plentiful food. I'm optimistic about the future because it's necessary to produce better food less destructively and growing food organically does that.'

5

The Changing Environment

Urbanization

Prague is one of the most expansive cities in the Czech Republic. Since the end of the Second World War (in 1945), the city has spread to include many villages that formerly surrounded it.

Large-scale expansion of urban housing took place in many other Czech cities during the 1970s and 1980s. As a project of the Communist government, thousands of people were housed in large blocks of flats called *panelaky*. Many of the panelak blocks were built close together in areas called *sidliste*, which means settlement. Most Czech people feel that these settlements are unattractive. Nowadays, *panelaky* are not built anymore, as people prefer to live in apartments or small family houses instead.

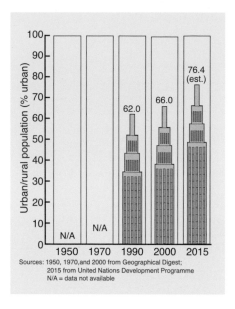

Sources: 1950, 1970, and 2000 from Geographical Digest;
2015 from United Nations Development Programme
N/A = data not available

▼ *The infamous* panelaky *of the Communist era are not being built anymore.*

▲ *It is estimated that more than three-quarters of Czech people will live in towns and cities by 2015.*

Noise pollution

The increasing traffic on the roads produces a lot of noise, especially along motorways and other main roads that are used by heavy lorries. In some areas, tall barriers have been raised to absorb the noise of the busy traffic.

Car ownership in the Czech Republic rose by 28 per cent from 1988 to 1992, however, from 1992 to 2003, this figure increased by another 30 per cent nationwide. In Prague alone the number of cars owned has doubled in the same period.

In response to the increased number of cars, some cities have introduced electric-powered trams and trolley-buses to provide more public transport. This has proved effective as there are fewer cars on the roads and less traffic noise and air pollution as a result.

▲ *Trams in Prague are a cheap and efficient way to get around the city.*

IN THEIR OWN WORDS

'My name is Michal Petrášek and I work for a German freight company, which transports goods all over Europe. Now that many people have access to the Internet they are able to shop across Europe, and transport companies are needed to deliver the goods. In the last few years our road system has grown. We are at the crossroads of East and West Europe and our government knows it's important to build motorways for the trucks that travel across the Czech Republic and other neighbouring countries. But, despite having more motorways, it is more difficult to get from place to place. Now there are a lot of traffic jams as more people own cars, and there are more trucks which slow down traffic.'

Air pollution

The main sources of air pollutants are the heat and power generating plants, that burn fossil fuels like coal and release masses of harmful particles from their chimneys into the atmosphere. These gases form great brown clouds called smog. Smog is very harmful to the environment and to people. The exhaust from cars, lorries and buses also contributes to smog pollution, especially in heavily populated areas with busy traffic. Air pollution on a global scale can cause a rise in the planet's temperature.

In the early nineties, after the regime change, the government emphasized the need to reduce emissions. By the year 2000 the Czech programme for the protection of the environment helped to reduce the levels of emissions by more than 50 per cent compared to 1990 levels. The Czech Republic has also signed a number of international agreements on anti-pollution laws as a contribution to a cleaner environment worldwide.

▲ *A gas-powered plant producing heating for flats. Gas-powered plants cause less pollution to the air than those powered by coal.*

◀ *Money is now being spent on restoring buildings damaged by air pollution.*

Water pollution

Most cases of water pollution happen when sewage plants and factories release chemical and biological waste into rivers. Sometimes contaminated rainwater can soak through the ground to the rivers and spread pollution further. This can make river and lake water dangerous for swimming in or drinking and certain fish species are becoming endangered. The government is working hard to prevent dangerous leaks and the levels of pollution have been decreasing since the late 1980s. However, the recent floods have been a setback. High water levels bring out oil from cars, flush the sewage systems and can disperse dangerous materials from flooded chemical factories.

► *The government is now tackling the problem of water pollution. Chemical pollution such as this is on the decrease.*

IN THEIR OWN WORDS

'My name is Roman Sušanka. There are many forests here and everyone likes nature but our environment was badly polluted by industrialization under communism. Now the government is trying to clean things up but this is very expensive. Many people just care about themselves, but young people with a bit more education care about the environment. In my school we have a biology group and carry out conservation projects.'

Recycling

The amount of waste materials created in the Czech Republic is increasing. In 2001 it produced nearly 45 million tonnes of rubbish. With larger amounts of waste it is becoming increasingly difficult to dispose of it. A lot of rubbish gets dumped in landfills. Unfortunately, this can pollute the soil and drain into underground water supplies. Another way of disposing of rubbish is to burn it in incinerators, but this can cause air pollution. A good way of solving the problem is to re-use waste materials in their recycled form. This requires separating waste products by type before they are collected for recycling. Specially designed containers for each type of rubbish have been introduced throughout the country. Disposing of waste in this way helps to contribute towards a better environment and cuts down the cost of new products.

▲ *Illegal dumping still occurs in the Czech Republic despite the changing attitudes towards environmental protection.*

◄ *Providing recycling bins in different colours makes it easier to sort rubbish out for recycling.*

IN THEIR OWN WORDS

'My name is Klára Volfová. Under the Communist government the environment wasn't considered to be important. However now our country is trying to improve the environment. One of the ways in which this is happening it to put a limit on tree cutting, and to plant more trees than are actually cut down. We can see many changes – before the Revolution nothing was recycled, but now the government has given us different coloured bins for different materials so that we can recycle our waste and learn how to protect our environment.'

Temelin power plant

The Temelin nuclear power station has been one of the major environmental safety concerns of recent years. The Russian and American-built reactor is supposed to be the best in its class. The government claims the reactor is safe, although the opening has been repeatedly postponed due to failed safety checks, and experts say that it is not as safe as modern Western reactors. Following the tragic accident at Chernobyl in the former Soviet Union, in the late 1980s, nobody wants to risk another disaster in the middle of Europe.

The Temelin plant is one of two Czech nuclear stations. The other, Dukovany, is operating without problems.

▼ *Steam rises from the cooling towers of the Temelin nuclear power plant during a test programme.*

6

The Changing Population

The population of the Czech Republic is currently estimated at just over ten million people. It had been growing slightly until 1993 when it reached its peak of just over 10.3 million. In 1993 the political changes of the late 1980s started to have a major effect on the Czech population. Before 1989, the average Czech couple brought up two children, which was more than in many Western European countries. By 1999 the number of babies born had dropped by nearly a half. This sharp drop was also experienced by other European post-Communist states like Hungary and Poland. The main reason for young Czechs having fewer children than in the Communist past is a mixture of economic uncertainty and more freedom of choice. People feel less secure about the future than they did before 1989. They also choose to spend more time pursuing their careers rather than bringing up a large family. Following the fall of the Soviet system, young people enjoy a wide choice of career, education and travel opportunities. They are experiencing the kind of freedom their parents could only dream of. But at the same time they know that having children is a commitment which takes a lot of these options away.

▲ *As the cost of living is becoming more expensive, parents often decide that having just one child is sensible.*

▶ *There are now many more large shopping centres than there were in the Communist era, which has given the people of the Czech Republic many more choices.*

The majority of young Czech people expect to live a similar lifestyle to people in the West but they can't always afford to do this. Many couples decide to have only one child. If the trend continues, the Czech Republic will have a growing number of elderly people. The government expects the situation to stabilize around 2010 but this depends on the country's economic and political position within Europe.

▶ *The number of elderly people in the Czech Republic is on the increase. This grandfather is looking after his grandchild, while the parents are at work.*

IN THEIR OWN WORDS

'My name is Milan Fait. I travel around the country selling pharmaceutical products. A big change here is that more people are getting divorced. Before the Revolution it was considered bad for couples to split up but now women have good well-paid jobs so they can leave and bring up children by themselves if they choose. My parents have been married for over 30 years and I'm very proud of that, but I know lots of young people who have divorced after only five years. People are also having fewer children now, and having them when they are older. My parents were in their twenties when they had me, but now women have children in their mid-thirties.'

Ethnic groups

The Czechs currently represent 94 per cent of the country's population. When the Czech Republic split from Slovakia in 1992, some Slovaks remained and represent roughly 3 per cent of the population. The other 3 per cent are mainly Polish, German, Roma and other ethnic groups. Most of the Roma people (also known as gypsies) are officially Czech but still use their own unique language.

Immigration

Before 1989, it wasn't as easy to travel in Europe as it is today. The political differences kept the East and the West well separated. Currently, there are large numbers of immigrants who travel across Europe, from East to West, in order to find a better life for themselves and their families.

People from poorer countries in Asia and Eastern Europe, such as Vietnam, Turkey, Ukraine, Moldavia, Romania, Russia and Bulgaria, travel to escape war or seek political asylum in more stable and peaceful countries. Before 1989, people came to former Czechoslovakia from Communist Vietnam as a part of a co-operation plan within the Communist group of countries. Many of them decided to stay and adopt Czech citizenship.

▲ A market stallholder of Vietnamese origin. The Vietnamese have been very successful with their markets, selling mainly tobacco, alcohol and clothes to tourists.

▶ A Roma woman in Olomouc selling magazines. The Roma community now has its own advisers who advise the national and local governments.

In Prague more than 5 per cent of the inhabitants are foreign citizens. Many are employees of the capital's foreign embassies and headquarters of companies that have business in the Czech Republic. Some immigrants have no money or travel documents and try to cross the borders illegally. The Czech Republic is becoming an increasingly popular destination for immigrants from the East, mainly because its central position in Europe makes it easier to travel to other countries.

▶ *A Nigerian student selling cruise tickets in Prague. The high standard of education in the Czech Republic attracts many foreign students, who take advantage of the relatively cheap university fees.*

IN THEIR OWN WORDS

'My name is Janis Tsolakidis. I am a student from Cheb. My mother's parents were from Slovakia and my father's from Greece. My grandfather was a Communist in Greece and when they lost the civil war there he had to flee here. There are quite a few Greek families who came at that time. There are several Vietnamese children in our school – it's difficult when there are several in a class because they speak Vietnamese to each other and don't join in with us. It doesn't matter what people look like, what's important is how they think and behave.'

7

Changes at Home

Family life

More than 70 per cent of Czech people live in apartments in urban areas. The usual family only has one or two children. Because of the housing shortage, most young adults continue to live with their parents until they can afford their own place. It is also common for the grandparents to live with their family. The grandmother, *babicka*, often plays an important family role and is looked upon with respect and love. A grandmother often lives with her children and looks after her grandchildren when both parents are at work.

▲ *Most Czech people still live in apartments, which are part of blocks like these. Many blocks built decades ago have been repainted and modernized to appeal to potential buyers.*

IN THEIR OWN WORDS

'I'm Jovana Janíková and I am a construction engineer and building inspector in Olomouc. Although there are many women engineers they usually do less well paid jobs than men. The main role of women in the Czech Republic is still to take care of the family. Many employers are afraid to employ women who have children in case they need to take time off work to care for their family. I think life is easier for single women who can build up their careers, especially in large cities. Childcare depends on the financial situation of the family – it's common to arrange for grandparents to look after children. I work freelance so I can take time off for my children.'

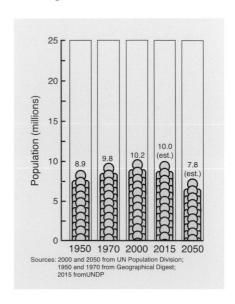

◄ *Military service is compulsory army training for all men who reach the age of 18. Most men complete this service before they marry, unlike in the past.*

▼ *The population in the Czech Republic peaked in 2000 and has begun to decline.*

In the past, Czechs tended to marry young, especially in rural areas. Young men often married before beginning military service at the age of 18. In communist times military service lasted two years but now it is just one. For young men who don't want to train in the army for personal reasons they can do alternative civilian service, which takes 18 months and involves various non-military work in public services. Today, people are marrying later in life. Some people have traditional village weddings with lots of singing, dancing and elaborate meals.

Many Czechs who live in cities also have weekend homes in the country where they have gardens and enjoy the outdoors with their families.

Religion

The most widespread religion in the Czech Republic is Roman Catholicism which currently includes 40 per cent of the population. Catholicism is especially popular in the Moravia region in the east of the country, where people of all ages attend church regularly. Pope John Paul II visited Moravia in 1990.

▲ *Catholicism is the most commonly practised religion. This picture shows St.Vitus Cathedral in Prague, the largest church in the country.*

The Czech Republic also has a well-established Jewish community, which consists of several thousand members. A synagogue in Prague has the names of more than 80,000 Czechoslovakian Jews who were killed in the Holocaust of the Second World War (1939-1945).

A large percentage of Czech people claim to be atheist (40 per cent). This is partly due to the fact that the Communist regime discouraged religion. The Communist Party leaders felt that religious people would be less likely to follow the socialist doctrine.

▶ *One of the two active synagogues in Prague. Many Jews from other countries come to see the synagogues.*

Education

The level of literacy in the Czech Republic is high at 99.9 per cent. Primary and secondary education in the Czech Republic is free for all children. Children start at the age of 6 and finish at 15 when they can choose to go on to higher education. Each primary school class has its own class teacher who is responsible for attendance and conduct. After the first two years, different teachers teach different subjects. Higher education used to be free in the Communist era but new economic conditions mean that now students have to pay for most of their college and university education. Another problem facing students is finding accommodation, as in the past that was organized by the government.

▼ *Pupils in Cheb leaving their secondary school in the afternoon. Most classes start at 8 o'clock in the morning from Monday to Friday.*

IN THEIR OWN WORDS

'My name is Jitka Juráčová, I work in the university library at Olomouc. I like reading and wanted to work with books. I did a special one year course for librarians. I then worked in a book shop for about ten years. Before the 1989 Revolution people were not able to read widely. Afterwards the books of Czech writers who had been prohibited were published. People wanted to read more and more, and to learn languages like English, French and German. For three or four years there was a big increase in reading and publishing. Before 1989 there were only three or four bookshops in Olomouc. After the Revolution there were about thirty. Now, however, there are about six, as most people prefer to watch TV than read a book. Many children are more interested in computers and computer games than reading.'

Changes in travel opportunities

In the Communist era the leisure activities of workers were massively subsidized by the government. People could easily afford to spend a nice holiday with their family but only in countries that were members of the Eastern Bloc, like Bulgaria or Hungary. Now there are no such restrictions. People can pursue what interests they like.

The increase of travel options has brought about a boom in the services industry. For example, before 1989 there was just one principal travel agency for the whole country. Older Czech people are now able to visit countries they could only dream of before. Travelling has also quickly become very popular with the young generation and today you can meet young Czechs who are travelling all over the world.

▲ *The cost of travelling abroad has gone down since 1989. The Czech National airline now flies people all over the world.*

◀ *Young people in Olomouc railway station. The price of tickets has gone up steeply in the past few years.*

Sports

Czech people are very keen on sports all year round. The most traditional sports are football and ice hockey. The Czech Republic ice-hockey team is one of the very best in the world. With the increase of Western influence after 1989 many new sports were introduced and the Czechs are keen on trying them out. Skateboarding became very popular with the younger generation and snowboarding offered an exciting alternative to the more traditional skiing. Other popular sports include tennis, volleyball and ice-skating.

▶ *Ice hockey is one of the most popular sports in the Czech Republic. Many people support the national team.*

IN THEIR OWN WORDS

'My name is Linda Nováková and I live in Cheb. In my free time I enjoy playing sports, going to a café for a drink or watching the television or a video. When my mother was young she spent her free time horse riding. She lived in a small village and life was very different for her as a girl as she had to help more in the home and garden. During the holidays I work as a camping instructor with children from the city. I love doing that. I also love travelling – I've been to Germany, Spain and Greece. We have a small chalet in the mountains and I go there for holidays.'

Diet

The diet and eating habits of the Czechs have begun to change as there is a wider choice and people are becoming aware of health issues. However, traditional foods are still very popular.

▲ *Restaurants are big business in Prague where eating out is becoming increasingly popular.*

The most popular option for eating out is still in public houses and restaurants where food and drinks are served at a table. Traditionally a large number of meat dishes will appear on menus. Eating meat, especially pork, is very popular in the Czech Republic. Roast pork side with pickled cabbage and sliced-up dumplings, or stewed beef goulash, are still loved and enjoyed by many Czechs today.

Since the changes in 1989, new influences and trends have appeared. New recipes and exotic foods are now available. There are several specialized tea shops in Prague, where you can buy different teas from around the world. Although the diet of the average Czech hasn't dramatically changed, there are some definite signs of an increasing focus on healthy eating. Health food shops selling organically grown produce is a new growth area.

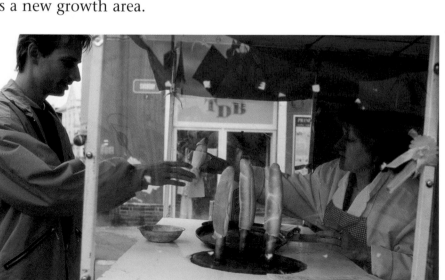

◄ *Fast food, like these hot dogs, is increasingly available and popular, although people are now becoming more aware of its negative impact on health.*

IN THEIR OWN WORDS

'I'm Hana Rudorferová. I have a shop selling organic foods, herbs and medicines. It has been here for ten years and is doing very well. Since the Revolution in 1989 people have become more interested in health foods. Before this no one knew about organic crops and health food shops were unheard of. Eating habits have changed enormously, and it's not only people's diet but also their attitude to life, and what they do with their free time. We live much healthier lives now in spite of working harder. Many people like me do exercises every morning, we eat less meat and drink a lot of water. In the past very few people were vegetarian but now it's widespread, especially amongst women.'

Health service

In the past, the quality of the health service in the Czech Republic had been very good compared to other European countries. In the Communist era all healthcare was paid for by the state. Nowadays people have to pay health insurance, except for children, the retired and the unemployed. After 1989 many hospitals and surgeries were privatized and became responsible for their own financing. Private surgeries charge patients when they come to see a doctor.

At present, the Ministry of Health is struggling to keep up the quality of healthcare because things are getting more expensive and the government is reluctant to increase spending on medical care.

◀ *A private clinic in Cheb. Private hospitals started functioning after 1989 and have been providing a good level of healthcare under the control of the Ministry of Health.*

Unemployment

Under Communist rule, people were guaranteed a job. Because of this it was very easy to get work, even for people with no skills, references or qualifications. This helped to keep the unemployment figures very low. The only social benefits that people took advantage of were maternity leave and sick pay, which were both paid for by the state. Nowadays jobs are much less secure and the levels of unemployment are rising.

One of the reasons why it is more difficult to get a job today is the situation in the housing market. The prices of houses are high and often it is not easy to find a suitable home that is close to work, so people struggle to find employment where it suits them. Some of the regions most affected by rising unemployment are in the north of the country where a lot of people work in the coal mining industry. When the miners worked under the Communist

▲ *Job security has decreased since 1989 and people have to make more effort to find a suitable job.*

▼ *Because many people are now coming to bigger towns looking for work, housing is becoming more of a problem, especially in cities such as Prague.*

IN THEIR OWN WORDS

'My name is Michal Kovář. Before the Revolution it was very hard to do what you really liked. You had to know the right people in the right places, and work was much less flexible – now it's easier to try something and, if it doesn't work out, to change. Now it's up to you what you do. I studied psychology but then gave that up and worked in a bookshop. Then I became interested in photography and am now writing reviews of digital cameras. The problem before the Revolution was that people didn't work so hard as they didn't benefit if they did. People expected the government to look after them. Many people are not used to running their own lives; they expect someone else to come and solve their problems. It will take time for people to get used to their new freedom.'

regime they were paid high wages. Now the miners still receive a good salary but in comparison to what they were earning their wages have been reduced and they are reluctant to take less well-paid jobs. Experts say that what is needed to help the unemployment-hit regions is to make them more accessible to investors from abroad. This would allow more businesses to develop and the number of job opportunities would increase.

◀ *These tram workers are fixing a rail junction. Working for the city council is usually a secure and well paid job.*

Tourist industry

Many people now work in tourism. After 1989, Prague quickly became the most visited capital of central Europe. Since then, Prague's reputation has grown and the Czech Republic has become well known for its culture and history.

The increased demand for accommodation has also boosted the Czech hotel industry. The quality and choice of hotel accommodation has improved since 1989.

It isn't just Prague that people come to see though. Many visitors are attracted by the beautiful scenery throughout the country, with wonderful architecture and well-kept castles. The western spa region is very popular with tourists for its abundance of cold and hot mineral springs, many of which have healing properties. The Czech Republic also offers affordable opportunities to pursue winter sports for visitors from Western Europe. Major tourist skiing centres are situated in the Krkonose Mountains in the north.

▲ *The Presidential Palace in Prague attracts many tourists from around the world.*

◄ *There are many shops in Prague selling traditional goods to tourists, such as this puppet shop.*

IN THEIR OWN WORDS

'I'm Karel Tříška and I'm 18. The biggest change for us is that now we can travel abroad. Before we could only go to countries like Hungary, the Soviet Union and Bulgaria, but now we can go everywhere.

Now in my school we use a lot of computers. A couple of years ago the government passed a law that all schools, primary and secondary, should have free Internet and computers. My school has two rooms with about 45 computers for 1000 students, aged 12 to 20. When I finish school I am hoping to work in computers.'

Computer industry

Until the early 1990s computers were available to only a few businesses. Now, computers have revolutionized working practices. The number of people having a computer at home and work has increased dramatically with the arrival of the Internet. Many new computer-related businesses have emerged including computer gaming and Internet cafés. People have quickly adapted to computers and they are becoming a part of everyday life, from use in shops to banking services.

▶ *There is public Internet access from this café. Access like this has become available since the late nineties.*

Changes in the economy

The Czech economy has recently undergone major transformations. Soon after the end of the Second World War (1945) it became obvious that Czechoslovakia was required to follow economic steps approved by the Soviet Union. After 1955 Czechoslovakia could no longer do business with the West.

Before 1989, almost all companies were owned by the state, which is typical for Communist countries. A transformation to a Western-style economy was needed in order for the Czech Republic to be able to function economically within Europe. A new stock market was established so that the shares of the privatized companies could be traded. Every person over the age of 18 years received their share of vouchers from the government. With these vouchers people were then able to buy shares in the privatized companies.

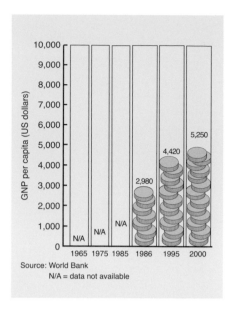

Source: World Bank
N/A = data not available

▲ *Since 1985 GNP (Gross National Product) has risen steadily.*

▼ *Since 1989, the ways that people handle their money have changed a great deal. For example, instead of going to the bank to withdraw money it can now be collected from the many cashpoints.*

IN THEIR OWN WORDS

'I'm Martin Hladeček and I have my own business which involves travelling around the country selling gas appliances and water heaters. Now we have more opportunities to travel and build our own careers. Businesses have contacts with the rest of the world. Life is much better now. I think of myself as a European and travel to other countries a lot – cheap flights have made this much easier. Our Republic is now visible and we are firmly on the map of Europe – in fact we are at the heart of Europe.'

The 'Skodovka'

The car manufacturer Skoda is a major Czech exporter. The factory, which is known as 'Skodovka', is situated in Mlada Boleslav in the north of the country and today it still employs thousands of people. The company is a good example of the transformation of Czech industry, which began after 1989. The recent political and economic changes in the Czech Republic have had a great effect on the company. As a part of the Soviet bloc, the Skoda factory was producing low quality cars that sold to the masses for a cheap price.

In 1991 the company was bought by their German counterpart, Volkswagen, and nowadays they produce quality cars which successfully sell in many other countries, including Germany, France and the United Kingdom.

▼ *Due to dramatic improvements in quality, Skoda remains the best selling car in the Czech Republic, despite competition from abroad.*

Women at work

Women and men in the Czech Republic, and previously in Czechoslovakia, always had equal opportunities in education and employment. Today, Czech women pursue higher positions much more than in the past. More women today have jobs as executives in companies, and work as government MPs, which is something that wasn't the norm in the Communist state. Although many women work full time outside the home, they are also responsible for housework and raising children. The state continues to provide generous maternity leave and social benefits for mothers, especially if they are single or have financial difficulties. With the ever-increasing pace of life, career options mean that many Czech women now decide to have children later in life so that they can concentrate on their career first.

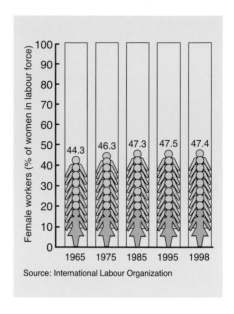

▲ Although the number of women in employment has remained constant since the 1960s there are more women in top jobs now than before.

◀ A woman surveyor at work. Czech women have equally good job opportunities as men.

Freedom of art

The art scene in general prospered greatly from the change of regime in 1989. Artists today enjoy real freedom, whereas in the Communist era the government always had control over what an artist produced. Anything that was not in accordance with the Communist idea could result in artists being prosecuted for betraying their country. Many artists who wanted to express themselves freely were imprisoned for undermining the government's authority. Among the many who refused to restrict their creativity was the former president of the Czech Republic, Vaclav Havel, who was imprisoned for many years for his satirical theatre plays.

▲ *Today's government doesn't put any restrictions on freedom of speech, so musicians can sing about what they like.*

IN THEIR OWN WORDS

'I'm Lukás Kosek and I work as a freelance visual designer for television commercials. Over the last ten years television advertising has changed a lot as we look to the West for our influences. Now television advertising is more professional and many foreign companies come here as it is cheaper.

After school I began to work in an advertising agency, doing graphic design. I didn't continue with further education because I knew what I wanted to do. Two years ago I came to Prague and worked at the film academy. I met a lot of people there who helped me with my work in the media.'

The Way Ahead

Between the two world wars (1918-1939), Czechoslovakia was a well developed country within Europe, both culturally and economically. The events of the Second World War (1939-1945) resulted in the political division of Europe. Although the west part of Czechoslovakia was liberated from German occupation by the US army in 1945, soon afterwards the whole country was firmly in the grip of the Soviet-controlled Communist government. From 1968 the country was occupied by the Russian armies until the fall of the Communist regime in the late 1980s. Under this repressive government many Czechs gave up trying to change things because it seemed like the Soviets were going to be in power forever.

▲ *Some traditions continue - the changing of the Castle Guard at Prague Castle.*

When the regime changed in 1989 people were surprised. The rapid changes in the economy, which followed, were a result of the effort to build up trade with the West again. This really put the new government to the test. The massive amount of state-owned capital was transformed into private businesses. This gave rise to many new businesses and foreign investors took the opportunity to join in.

Many older people have forgotten about the past disadvantages of the Communist system and are

► *An example of Prague's modern architecture – the Dancing House.*

◄ *Most young students are confident about their chances of success in the future.*

disappointed because everything has become so expensive. However, before 1989, when people wanted to buy something they had to wait in a long queue and even then might not get what they wanted. Overall, the Czech people find the new system much better. The freedom to do or say what they like cannot be measured by money. Despite various setbacks, the prospects for the economy are good and there are more opportunities for an exciting and varied life.

IN THEIR OWN WORDS

'My name is Tereza Hercigová. I hope we will join the European Union and things will improve. It will give us more opportunities to live and work abroad. Some people are afraid that prices will go up, and are suspicious of foreigners. Communism was very bad for this country because everything belonged to the state so no one really cared about the shops and factories. It didn't matter how well or badly anyone worked because they were paid anyway. This attitude needs to change and people have to work harder. If we do, our future will be bright.'

Glossary

Acid rain Heavily polluted rain of high acidity which is very harmful to the trees.

Adriatic Sea Part of the Mediterranean Sea between Italy and the Balkans.

Baltic Sea This lies between the coasts of Germany, Poland and Scandinavia.

Communism A political system in which the government controls all production and which has no different social classes.

Eastern Bloc Countries of Eastern Europe which had Communist governments and supported the Soviet Union.

Ecological The relationship between people and the environment.

Emissions Gasses or other substances which a factory produces and releases into the air.

Environmentalist A person who is engaged in activities aimed at the protection, preservation and research of the natural environment.

Federation A system of government in which two or more states unite into one country.

Hydro power Electricity generated by turbines that are turned by the force of falling water.

Holocaust The killing of Jews in Europe by the Nazis in the 1940s.

Moravia Eastern region of the Czech Republic where people speak a distinctive dialect of Czech.

MP Member of Parliament, an elected representative of the people.

Organic food All food grown without the use of artificial methods and fertilizers which therefore doesn't contain any harmful ingredients.

Satirical play A play which deliberately makes the subject (for example, politicians) seem funny to show its faults.

Soviet Elected council in a Communist country (Soviet Union).

Subsidy Money that is paid by a government to reduce the cost of producing goods.

Synagogue A building where Jewish people meet for religious worship.

Further Information

Books for younger readers
Country Insights: Czech Republic by Rob Humphreys
(Wayland, 2006)

Czech Republic (Picture a Country) by Henry Pluckrose
(Franklin Watts, 2001)

Books for older readers
Prague in Black and Gold: The History of a City by
Peter Demetz (Penguin Books,1998)

Useful addresses
British Embassy
Thunovská 14
118 00 Prague 1
Tel: 257 402 111
Fax: 257 402 296

Agency for nature conservation and landscape
protection of the Czech Republic
Kalinsňická 4-6
130 23 Prague 3
email plesnik@nature.cz

Index

Page numbers in **bold** refer to photographs, maps or statistics panels.